Product Research 101: Find Winning Products to Sell on Amazon and Beyond

Renae Clark

Disclaimer

The content in this book is intended to be educational and informational in nature. The author and publishers make no claims or guarantees of income. We are not lawyers or accountants and the information in this book does not substitute for advice from a qualified professional. You are responsible for evaluating whether the techniques in this book are appropriate for your business. This includes doing your own due diligence.

Table of Contents

Introduction

Just getting started with product research and sourcing? Stuck trying to find ideas or find that "perfect" winning product? Want to find good selling products that others are ignoring? Interested in wholesale or private label products? If you answered yes, then this book is for you.

If you are an experienced seller or are looking to do arbitrage this book will have less value as I don't discuss sourcing by arbitrage. I don't do arbitrage, so I don't teach it. This book is written for the new or struggling seller wanting to source wholesale or private label products.

What you will learn:

- Basic steps for finding top selling products

- How to generate product ideas and look for trends

- How to validate demand

- Tips for finding suppliers

- Analyzing data to help you pick a product

It took me 5 months of research before I pulled the trigger on my first products to sell on Amazon. Five months and countless hours. I have pages of notes with product ideas in many different categories. Some were wholesale products; others were ideas for my own products. I had some money set aside to buy inventory. But I couldn't commit. I was looking for...not necessarily *thee* perfect product, but, well yeah, the perfect product.

Fear of choosing "wrong" was holding me back. I knew that product selection was key to success so I needed to choose right. Another part of the problem was I had bigger ideas—I wanted to create a brand and I had some ideas as to what sorts of products I would carry. But those ideas required more capital than I was willing to invest for my first product. As a result, I put so much pressure on myself to dream big and think towards the future that I did...nothing!

Another hold up was I was a little skittish to follow the advice to source from Chinese suppliers. It seemed so complicated for a beginner. Could I not take a little less profit and source domestically? Were there not manufacturers that could produce my ideas in North America? Yes, and yes.

Ultimately the delays helped me because I learned a lot by joining Facebook groups and listening to and learning from the experiences of others. I devoured the advice in forums as well as blogs, books, webinars, and courses. I learned of the pitfalls of private label that the gurus selling you the dream never talk about. And finally, I did pull the trigger.

I put together this guide to help any of you who are feeling a little gun-shy too. I put this book together for all of you who have the brains to say "Hey, if everyone buys top 100 selling products won't that saturate the market?" I put this book together to help you find great products from many different approaches. After reading this, you should feel confident enough to find a product and get started with your e-commerce business.

Chapter 1: Getting Started

Let's cut to the chase, selling on Amazon is hot right now. With increased numbers of sellers, there is more competition. More competition means that finding the right products to sell has become trickier. Selecting the products that will make you money can be stressful. Amazon fees can easily eat away profits making proper product selection even more crucial.

This is a business where you need to spend money to make money. Unlike affiliate marketing, blogging, or writing eBooks, the investment is a little bigger on the front end. The more inventory you have, the greater potential for sales. However, the more inventory you have, the more money you have tied up in inventory. When you are first starting out and have a limited budget this increases the pressure to spend wisely.

We all want that winning product right out of the gate—you know, the one everyone else seems to have but you can't seem to find. The public can be fickle so predicting success is no more than an educated guess. What's hot today can be a closeout next week. What we need to do is make that educated guess and then test the market with that product. If it does well you can invest more money in that product and then work on finding your next product. Soon you will have a nice catalog of products that perform well for you.

If you haven't studied much about Amazon FBA, I will walk you through what I call the Best Sellers Strategy for sourcing. Almost any book or course about FBA teaches this method. It is a valid method but the problem is that with everybody taking this approach the products here are quickly getting saturated with sellers. I want you to be able to find ideas for products in other ways. Products that can do well with less competition because they live just off the radar. I have edited this book to be as concise and actionable as possible. You should be able to read it in one evening and get sourcing right away. Let's get started.

Before you start, know where you want to go

It can be helpful to consider what kind of goals you have so that you make decisions that align with your bigger picture. Sure, ultimately we all want to give the boot to our day job and work from home but for the majority of us, this doesn't happen overnight. Instead, think about what you want to achieve in the next 6-12 months. Write it down—it could be in terms of a monetary goal or some other milestone. Examples might include:

"I want to net $500 a month from my Amazon business"

"I want to be able to take my family to Disneyland"

"I want to have launched my own product that sells 5 units a day"

"I want to be working no more than 3 days a week at my day job"

Closely tied to these goals is your motivation. Why do you want to do e-commerce? Are you looking for a side income? A replacement income? Are you looking for a career change? Do you have a passion to bring a certain product to the market?

What does all this self-reflection have to do with product sourcing? Knowing your motivation will help you make decisions in your business. If you want to bring a certain product to market you may have already have identified a niche and will ultimately want to private label or custom manufacture your products. If you are doing this solely for the income you may be willing to sell whatever product can turn a quick profit. Before you make any major purchase decision, weigh it against your goals and motivation. Does the decision bring you closer to your goals? Is the decision in line with why you are in this business?

Once you start investing in inventory your money is tied up until those products sell. My first products on Amazon were some wholesale items that I knew could sell and were easy to acquire. I quickly realized that not only were my margins slim on these products, but that my capital was tied up until they sold. Ultimately I wanted to bring my own line of products to the market and doing random wholesale items was slowing my progress by tying up funds. I decided I needed to stick to the niche I wanted to be in and stay focused on my end goal. You need to evaluate your situation. If you have little startup money, you may need to sell whatever you can at first in order to raise more startup money and that is fine. The point is to know where you want to go before you start. Without focus you will be tempted to chase every lead that seems half promising. You will get where you want to be much faster if you stay focused on your goals.

Using your goals as a guide, give some thought to how you plan to source your products. Many successful sellers begin by scouring retail and online sources for bargains (including garage sales and thrift stores) and flipping them for a profit. This can be a great way to start if you have little capital to invest and want to raise funds. Arbitrage, as this technique is referred to, is not part of the scope of this book as it is a world unto itself. If you want to do arbitrage to get started, I recommend Chris Green's book of the same name. The focus here is sourcing wholesale and private label products.

What is Wholesale?
Wholesale is buying in bulk quantities at a discounted price and then selling at retail price. The advantages and disadvantages (relative to private label) of selling products that you purchase wholesale are:

Pros

- Choosing products that already have a good sales rank and good reviews will reduce customer complaints and when combined with FBA will help you achieve a positive seller rating

- Products with good sales rank already turn up high in the search results versus a new to market or a new to Amazon product

- Usually able to source domestically

- Some wholesalers have minimum dollar orders instead of minimum units so you can mix and match products. This allows you to build a wide catalog of many products versus a small catalog where you are deep in just a few products. A wider catalog minimizes the risk of slow moving inventory

- Can create unique listings by bundling

- Help you to learn/understand the FBA process without a large investment in a single product

- Get ungated in restricted categories (such as beauty or grocery) with wholesale invoices from your suppliers

Cons

- Some wholesalers do not want eBay or Amazon sellers as customers

- Margins may be thin—some wholesale prices don't leave much room for profit after shipping and Amazon fees are deducted

- You share the listing with other sellers which means:

  - Compete for the buy box—more competition based on price

- More competition = slower moving inventory if you don't have the buy box

- May compete with Amazon and their bulk buying power (it can be hard to compete with Amazon on price)

What is Private Label?

Private Label (also called White Label) is contracting a manufacturer to make a product for you. This can be taking an existing product that they already make and putting your name on the packaging, or you can have them customize one of their products according to your specifications. If you think of the house brand at your local supermarket, or Target's Archer Farms this is private label in action. Even Trader Joe's works largely on the private label model—sourcing products from all over the world and contracting the manufacturer to make them for Trader Joes.

Pros

- You create the listing—it is as good as you make it

- You are the only seller on the listing so no competition for the buy box (but see first con below)

- You create a brand identity that can help market future products

- Higher profit margin potential

Cons

- If your product is not sufficiently unique, others with the same product can sell on your listing. This might happen if you buy a generic product without customizing it in any way.

- You start from ground zero. You need to do the marketing and hustle to get legitimate reviews on your listing. You need to promote your product through free and paid means to drive traffic to your listing.

- Usually requires higher minimum orders of a single unit which means a lot of money invested in a sink or swim product.

As we move on to the process of researching products to sell, if you are looking for products to wholesale you will be looking for *specific products* that already exist (e.g. an Omron blood pressure wrist cuff) that you can find wholesale sources for. If you are looking to private label, you will be looking for successful products to be inspired by (not copy!!). You will be looking at what *types* of products sell, such as wrist style blood pressure cuffs.

When looking for private label products you should pay attention to reviews—what do people love about the product, and more importantly what do they hate that you can improve upon. For example, you may decide to create a wrist blood pressure cuff with large easy to read numbers that is lightweight or rechargeable based on your research of what customers want.

Chapter 2: Gather Ideas

Goal: Choose a few potential categories and generate lists of potential products within those categories.

The first step is to find one or more starting points. We need to narrow down the millions of potential products to a healthy list of candidates.

Writers often free write when starting a new project. The idea is to write down whatever comes to mind without censoring or editing it. The first place to start any project is to gather a good list of ideas. I think you will find that once the ideas start to flow, you won't be able to turn off the tap. If you do get stuck, don't worry, I have a whole list of suggestions that will stimulate the flow. I recommend keeping a notebook with you at all times (or install something on your smartphone that allows you to make notes).

While you should write down anything that seems like it might be a good product or idea, I want to give you your first set of filters at the outset. Eliminating products that don't meet these criteria out of the gate will keep your list from get unmanageably long and make your job of validating ideas (Chapter 3) easier. Bear in mind that these criteria apply when you plan on using Amazon's fulfillment services (FBA). You have more latitude if you store and ship your own inventory because you won't have the extra fulfillment fees.

Initial criteria for product selection:

Selling price over $10. Selling prices under $10 are best merchant fulfilled or you will struggle to make a profit. Amazon FBA fees usually start at around $3.50 and go up from there. The FBA fee is based on a fixed pick and pack fee (roughly $2) as well as a variable weight fee. Amazon takes about 15% of the selling price in commission on top of that (varies by category but 15% is the most common). You must also factor in the cost to send the item to Amazon's warehouse, which could add $0.25-0.75 per item to your cost, depending on weight. You could easily pay $5 in fees on a single item. In order to make a 20% profit on a $10 item your cost to acquire the item needs to be around $3. You can see how you are working on slim margins here with little room for error and even less room to adjust your price if your competitors start underpricing you.

Small and light. Your shipping costs to Amazon as well as your weight based FBA fee will be less on lighter items. Oversized items are allotted less space (every seller has an allotment of warehouse space) which may limit the number of products you can have in inventory. Small and light is not a mandatory filter—you make the call. There may be instances where a larger product may have less competition because everyone else is looking for small and light. I do recommend that you strongly consider weight and size for your first product or two until you get a handle on fees. You wouldn't want to send in 20 oversized teddy bears only to discover that the fees eat all of your profits (ask me how I know!).

Not a hazardous material, or anything remotely resembling one. Amazon has a huge list of products that can't participate in the FBA program (but can still be merchant fulfilled). Don't memorize them but do read over the list so you have an idea what is not allowed. Examples include aerosols, flammable liquids, batteries, and cleansers. For a more complete list of examples of hazmat products see Selling at Amazon.com>Fulfillment by Amazon>FBA Policies and Requirements>FBA Product Restrictions> Hazardous Materials Identification Guide>Which Amazon Products Might Be Hazmat? Don't take for granted that just because others are selling it by FBA that you can too. Some sellers have permission to sell certain hazmat items via FBA. If you are set on selling something hazmat you need to be willing to merchant fulfill these items.

Non-perishable. I think this is good advice for beginners because while you are learning the ropes, you don't want to worry about selling your product before it expires. Items with no expiry date may sit on the shelf awhile, but eventually they sell and you will get your money out of them. Perishables such as grocery or beauty products can be great because people need to purchase them over and over, but I don't recommend it as first product. If it gets close to expiration you will not be permitted to sell it and will either have to pay to have it returned to you or pay Amazon to destroy it. Once you have a better feel for what sells and how quickly you will be able to select perishables with confidence.

Not fragile. Items that are easily broken means a higher return rate and negative reviews. You can't afford this when you are new. If you have four 5 star reviews and one negative review, that's an 80% feedback rating—yipes.

Not a lot of moving parts or electronics. Again, don't choose something easily broken until you get enough positive feedback built up. Even then, make sure you package it well!

As you brainstorm ideas, don't get hung up on finding a single niche or category to sell in. Many Amazon sellers have products in multiple categories. Selling on Amazon is different than having your own e-commerce website where customers expect to see a theme. You could list 20 different products in 15 different categories and it wouldn't matter. You can always specialize later as you discover what products work best for you. So, as you go through this idea phase write everything down that seems plausible. We will research and validate later, so at this point just look for ideas. First, give yourself 10 minutes and write down everything that comes to mind.

When you are done, move on to the following suggestions to find more ideas.

Your timeline for generating ideas is up to 1 week initially, but make this an ongoing project. After 1 week, move on to validation. You do not want to get stuck in this phase. You can always be adding potential ideas to your notebook. In fact, you will notice yourself finding potential opportunities everywhere!

Narrow the field to a few categories or markets

Browse. Browse through the categories and see what appeals to you. What kind of categories or niches interest you? Don't think broad top level categories like Home and Kitchen but choose a subcategory like Arts and Crafts or even more specifically, scrapbooking. Write down 3-5 niche areas that you are interested in. Remember, you are not married to any of these, the goal here is to narrow the field from millions of possible products down to thousands.

Your profession. Think about your professional knowledge. Are there any tools or supplies you use in your workplace? Chances are you already know where to source them, so this might be a good category for you.

Your hobbies. What do YOU spend money on? Think about any hobbies or interests you have. I know that every time I pick up a new hobby or interest I end up spending a bunch of money getting all the tools and supplies I need. The more you know and are passionate about what you are selling, the better you will be able to sell it to others. A seller who is knowledgeable can intelligently answer questions about their products, and a seller who is passionate about what they are selling will be able to write compelling descriptions, not to mention sourcing will be fun!

The essentials. What do you use every day? Items that people need to buy over and over again can be a great product to invest in. Sometimes the most mundane product can be the most profitable. I knew someone once with a million-dollar business...making window screens. It's not glamourous but almost every home has them. Your product does not need to be sexy. If you can make a profit selling curtain rods or shower rings, why not?

Look around your house, your garage, your car. What products do you not want to be without? My two favorite kitchen tools are my vegetable peeler and chef's knife. Everything else is gadgets, but if anything happened to those two tools, I would need to replace them right away. What can you not be without?

Solve a problem. What do you wish existed or could be better (half the time if you look hard enough, someone has already come up with that product—but if not, you could be the one to get it made). Think of the person who invented the car stop. Every time I drop a French fry between the seat and console of my car I think, damn, I need one of those things (I eat in my car a lot). What need or frustration can you solve?

Think local. Think about the area where you live. Are there any product manufacturers or wholesale companies within driving distance? This could be a great way to save money on shipping which reduces your cost of goods and thereby increases your margins. What products do these companies sell? I know I have one company near me that makes supplements as well as a couple of tool wholesalers. I would not have ordinarily thought to sell in these markets.

Use the ideas you generate from the above to choose 3-5 markets or niches that you are interested in. Remember, over the long haul you are not married to these categories but rather we are trying to narrow down the choices for your initial products.

Generate a list of products within those categories or markets

The purpose of choosing some categories or niches is to give you a starting point for identifying products to sell. By narrowing the field to a few niches searching becomes more manageable. Start with one category on your list and create a list of products. Repeat as needed with each category on your list. You may have already generated some product ideas while brainstorming niches. Be sure to include them.

Follow any or all of the suggestions below, writing down product ideas as you go. At this point we are not looking to source, so just write down product ideas that strike your fancy and meet most of the criteria above.

Tip: Start an Excel spreadsheet to list your ideas in. As you move on to validation you can add columns to it for fees, price, number of competitors, etc.

The Best Seller Method. I recommend starting on Amazon itself and browsing the top 100 bestsellers in your category as well as subcategories under it. But wait you say, I thought we were going to learn something different? Bear with me, this is just the beginning. You should write down anything interesting, but more than that you are looking to get an idea in your head as to what sorts of products are bestsellers in your category. Are they staples, everyday items, unique items, tools, supplies? How would you characterize the top items in your category? You can "category down" (i.e. sub-categories) 2-3 times before being in the top 100 starts to lose its meaning in terms of fast moving items (for example, what does it mean to be in the top 100 of the subcategory "transfer pipettes")

Point to remember: The Bestseller list is fluid and changes often. In fact, sales rank really just equates to how recently that product was last sold. If a bestselling item doesn't sell for a few days (maybe it is out of stock) it can quickly slip from the Bestseller's list. A product may be in the top 100 due to seasonal popularity (e.g. Halloween, pool supplies) or because it was featured in a magazine or blog post. It may be in the top 100 because a promotion or giveaway was recently run. That's why later we will verify with some web tools that these products have a good sales history. If you are wanting to private label a potential bestselling product, consider tracking its sales rank for several weeks before pulling the trigger on anything more than samples.

Tip: Choose a category and type [ ] (with a single space in between the brackets) in the search bar. This will load all the products in that category. Consider sorting by average customer review to find the best rated products. If there are lots of reviews, you know it has been selling because fewer than 5% of customers actually leave a review and you will do yourself the favor of finding products that people love.

Don't forget to check the Movers and Shakers as well as the Hot New Products Lists for each of your categories. These lists live on the right side of the page when you view the Best Sellers list.

When you click on a product page, scroll down and look at the section "Customers who bought this item also bought." Many sellers use this section to generate ideas for bundles, but you may also find hidden gold by sourcing the products that frequently sell *with* a best seller instead of selling the best seller itself.

I believe that sourcing exclusively from the Top 100 Best Sellers is not the best strategy. I do believe in sourcing some bestsellers but the competition is too fierce at the top. I believe that a better long term strategy is to have a diverse catalog of products. I share some thoughts about the pros and cons of sourcing directly from the Bestsellers list in Appendix A.

Now that you have an idea about what kinds of things are popular, let's think outside the box. The fact is that everyone learning to do Amazon FBA has been taught to look at the best sellers. We want to find good selling products just outside of that list that your competition is not finding because they are fixated on the Top 100.

If you think you need to find a bestseller, think again. The Chrome extension Jungle Scout (which helps you analyze products) publishes a tool that correlates sales rank with number of sales per day. You can enter a rank and it will estimate the number of sales per day for all of the main categories. You will be surprised at how high a rank you can go in Home and Kitchen and still sell roughly 10 units a day. There are plenty of products that sell well that are not on the bestsellers list.

Ways to find great products beyond the Top 100

FBA Toolkit. Go to www.fbatoolkit.com, which is a free tool, and click on a category from the home page (you may need to register, but do not need to buy a plan). You will get a list of all of the products in that category that they are tracking sorted by sales rank. They are not tracking every single product so beware that some products may get skipped. Start browsing through the pages. This may take a while, but go deep. I usually start at a rank of around 500 and not even bother with 1-500 because of the high competition. Remember, in some categories you can go as high as 5000-10,000 sales rank in a top level category and still find good selling items. In fact in Office Products, the top 1% of products is ranked under 60,000. The top 1% of products in Automotive is ranked under 133,000.

FBA toolkit tries to estimate the number of sales of an item for the last 30 days however many sellers feel that their data is not that accurate. Don't count on FBA Toolkit so much for data, but rather use it as a way to browse by rank well beyond the top 100.

How to use this tool for research:

Browse products by ascending rank to search beyond the Top 100

Social Shopping. Browse social shopping sites. Woot is a daily deals site where the community gives feedback on products. You can check the sales stats for the products offered on their site including sales per day and sales per hour as well as how long it took before the first person bought it. Groupon and Living Social are other sites that offer daily deals. There are tons of these sorts of sites and you can find both local and national ones at http://localdealsites.com/

Other social shopping sites (such as Fancy.com) allow users to submit finds. Users can browse and upvote these products. On Fancy, you can browse the most popular products in each category as well as check out how many people "fancied" the items. Other sites like Fab.com have a section for what is trending. Take some time to browse a few of these social shopping sites in your potential categories.

How to use these sites:

Use them to find out how many of a deal have sold. Most deals are short term so you can see which items or which types of items sell a lot and sell quickly.

Use them to check feedback on the product

On social shopping sites where shoppers submit the products, look for what has been voted up or shared a lot.

Check which products are trending

Niche E-commerce Websites: Go to niche online retailers for a niche or category that you have on your list. Select a category on that site and sort by "Popularity." If that is not an option try sorting by "Bestselling" or "Highly rated." I recommend checking "Highly rated" regardless because you want a product that will get good reviews. Try a few different online stores and find out what is selling on those sites specifically. For example, if you want to sell camera accessories go to B & H Photo and find your category, for example camera bags. Once you get a list of products in that category, sort by Bestselling and also by Top Rated.

Caution: Some niche online stores may carry specialized items for that niche that some people may not even think to look for on Amazon. For example, certain jewelry tools might be very popular on a jewelry supply store but rank poorly on Amazon. Bestselling is relative to all of the other products *on that site*. In the next chapter we will talk more about validating the product for the Amazon marketplace.

You can use this same strategy with big box online retailers like Target.com, Walmart.com, Wayfair.com, BestBuy.com etc. Pick a category and then sort the results by Popularity, Bestselling, and Best Rated. Once you have the results, browse the first few pages for ideas.

How to use these sites:

Use this technique to find out what is selling well elsewhere. If you are selling to a niche market, you are gathering data from where that niche market shops. You are also seeing what established retailers in a niche think is worth offering for sale.

Viral Posts and Social Proof. Go to Pinterest and search keywords related to your niche to find blog posts rounding up new and interesting products. An example might be 'best baking tools' or 'baking tools 2015' Read through some of these roundup posts to find unique ideas. Write down any that look interesting. You can do the same keyword searches on Google but on Pinterest you can see what posts are popular based on the number of re-pins. With Pinterest you get ideas and social proof in one fell swoop.

Other keywords to try on Pinterest or Google are "must have" "hot" and "trending" plus your category such as kitchen gadgets, education toys, iPhone accessories, etc. For example, "must have kitchen gadgets" or "hot iPhone accessories."

Tip: Search these same keywords on www.buzzsumo.com. This site will show you the posts that have been the most viral across all major social media platforms for those keywords.

How to use these sites:

Find recommended products by bloggers in your niche area

Find hot or trending products based on social proof (number of shares, pins, etc.)

Keyword Search Tools. Go to Google Keyword Planner and search for "buy" keywords like 'best kitchen knife' and see what related keywords come up. What is a buy keyword? Think about if you were going to buy that product--what terms would you search for? "Best" and "Reviews" are two common buy keywords. Use this information to find long tail search terms that can generate product ideas. For example, if you search "SLR camera bags" and you notice there are 150 monthly searches for "SLR camera bag orange polka dots" you may find yourself in the position of being the only seller of orange polka dotted camera bags with nary a competitor in sight. You may say, but wait, that is such a small search volume. Yes, it is, but if you have all 150 potential customers per month to yourself it may be worth it. If you also carry the pink and blue polka dotted camera bags you may have 450 potential customers per month.

A paid keyword option is Merchant Words. This web tool will give you keyword search volumes based solely on Amazon searches

(Google Keyword Planner is reporting search volume for the internet in general). You can use Merchant Words for free on a limited basis. Type in your keyword and then sort by 'search volume' to get the top 3 results. A subscription will get you full results.

Keyword Tool Dominator will do a similar job but displays all keyword results. The downside is it gives you results with a popularity score of 0-10 instead of search volume. The most popular keywords are ranked 0 while the least popular are assigned a 10. Keyword Tool Dominator allows a limited number of daily searches for free. Keyword Tool Dominator also will perform keyword searches for Etsy, Google Shopping, and eBay.

Use Trade Show Directories. Find trade shows in your niche or category and look at the list of exhibitors on the trade show's website. Visit the websites of any companies that sound interesting and see what products they carry. ASD is one of the largest general trade shows in the United States. Their exhibitor directory is at http://www.asdonline.com/exhibitor-directory.shtml. The Canton Fair is a huge trade show in China. You can browse their exhibitors at http://www.e-cantonfair.com/

Look for other niche trade shows like toy shows, clothing shows, etc. Conduct a Google search for your niche plus "trade show" or "gift show." You can also find a directory of major trade shows at https://www.greatrep.com/TradeShows.aspx

How to use this method:

Use these options to find new and unique products that may not be on Amazon already. Bringing a product onto Amazon has similar disadvantages as private label in terms of getting the product ranked, but you will be the only seller for a period of time. Use your knowledge from browsing the top selling categories to predict what might be popular.

Spy on eBay. Search www.watchcount.com to see what is hot on eBay. Search by keyword to get specific product ideas or just browse by category. eBay appeals to a different market than Amazon so just because something is hot on eBay, it doesn't guarantee that it will do well on Amazon. You can certainly use it, however, to get some ideas and validate them for Amazon later.

How to use this site:

Use this site to find hot sellers on eBay.

Do a keyword search to find specific product ideas

Browse magazines and newspapers. My local Seattle Times has a Marketplace section every weekend that highlights hot and interesting products with a theme. Examples would be five bags for the beach, or antiaging cosmetics, or hiking shoes. Other sources for these sorts of roundups include print magazines. Prevention magazine has a section each month highlighting health and beauty products, usually organized by a theme such as five moisturizers with Vitamin C. Prevention will also sometimes have grocery themed roundup articles featuring top product picks like best frozen diet meals, or best grab and go snacks (remember that Grocery is a gated category for Amazon sellers so you will need approval first). Sometime these lists include some smaller brands, which may present an opportunity for you to find an up and coming product.

How to use this:

Similar to looking for viral blog posts, use magazines and newspapers to gather product ideas within a certain niche or category

Watch TV. Go to the Home Shopping Network (or similar) website and browse your desired category. Filter by bestselling, customer picks, and best rated to find products that customers are buying and loving. Watch home shopping channels to see what sort of products sell quickly and use them for inspiration.

How to use this:

This technique is similar to perusing the social shopping sites. You are looking for what sells, how quickly, and in what volume.

By now you will hopefully have a healthy list of product ideas to work with that meet most of our preliminary criteria. If you don't, you can go back and repeat the process with one or more of the other categories you came up with at the outset. Otherwise, let's move on to researching these products a little further and validating whether they are indeed good product choices.

Chapter 3: Validation

Goal: Narrow the list of product ideas to those that perform well on Amazon and have reasonable competition

In the first steps, we were looking to generate a list of product ideas. We had our initial set of filters but otherwise did not censor our list. Now we need to research the potential of these products on Amazon. The purpose of validating these ideas is to evaluate

- How well do these products sell on Amazon?

- How many competitors are there? For wholesale this means how many sellers are on the product listing? For private label this means how many similar products are there? We want to make sure there is room for us to get a slice of the sales.

Gated Categories and Restricted Brands

The first thing I want you to do is figure out which products might belong to gated categories. Don't cross these products off your list, just put a G next to them for Gated. One day you may decide to get approval to sell in that category and you will have a head start with product ideas. Beware that there is a lot of category confusion in the Amazon catalog. Items may belong to categories you wouldn't logically expect, or worse, shady sellers may list a gated product in an open category and hope to get away with it.

As of publication, the categories requiring approval to sell in are:

3D Printed Products

Automotive & Powersports

Beauty

Clothing & Accessories

Collectible Books

Collectible Coins

Entertainment Collectibles

Fine Art

Gift Cards

Grocery & Gourmet Foods

Health & Personal Care

Independent Design

Industrial & Scientific (still on the official list but rumored to be open as of this publication)

Jewelry

Luggage & Travel Accessories

Major Appliances

Services

Sexual Wellness

Shoes, Handbags & Sunglasses

Sports Collectibles

Textbook Rentals

Video, DVD, & Blu-ray

Watches

Wine

To see the requirements to get approval to sell in these categories, navigate to Selling at Amazon.com>Policies and Agreements>Category, Product, and Listing Restrictions>Categories and Products Requiring Approval and click on View Requirements.

If you are planning to sell wholesale merchandise, you should also check what brands are restricted. This means you must be authorized by the manufacturer to be a reseller for those products on Amazon. There are many unofficial lists of restricted brands on the internet such as at http://www.meganwillifordonline.com/brands-that-are-restricted-to-sell-on-amazon-fba/. These are largely compiled from community input and not necessarily complete.

You can also check for restricted products by starting the listing process on Seller Central for any product that you have your doubts about. Do not let it go live, but check to see if you get any warnings during the listing process before investing in that product. Just because other sellers are selling it does not mean that it is not restricted. Those sellers may be authorized by the brand to sell that product.

I recommend that you bookmark the gated categories page as well as one or two restricted brands lists on your computer so you can refer back to them quickly. While these lists may seem to really restrict the field, there are millions of other products. Remember your mama telling you there are plenty more fish in the sea? She was right.

Validation steps
Now that we have a little smaller list to focus on, let's start validating products. What do I mean by validation? We are going to check sales rank, competition, and price history to see if this is a good product to invest in.

As you validate, you may want to open all of the tools mentioned below as tabs in your browser and work product by product. This way you can gather all the needed data at once rather than jump around.

Check Rank

For Amazon, sales rank means sales velocity. Any product's sales rank is a reflection of how recently it sold. Therefore, an item that sells many per day will have a lower rank while an item that sells once a week will have a higher rank.

From your list, find each product on Amazon and determine its sales rank. You can find this information by clicking on the Product Page and scrolling down to the Product Details section.

Most sellers are looking for products in the top 1%, top 3% or top 5% of a top level category (such as Home & Kitchen in this example). You can check this web page (http://www.mysilentteam.com/public/Amazon-Categories-Decision-Helper.cfm) for a chart that is updated periodically. You can also calculate it yourself.

To calculate sales rank percent yourself, navigate to your category and put [ ] in the search field (put a single space between the open and closed brackets) and press Enter. In the top left corner, it will show the total number of results in that category.

For any given product divide the sales rank number for the product by the total number of products in that category.

In the example above 13,535/55064769 is 2.45 or .02% which means the product is well within the top 1% for that category.

What rank should you be aiming for? There are 200 million+ products on Amazon so if you are in the top 1% you are in the top 2 million products. The closer you are to the top 1%, the more sales volume you will have but also more competition. More competition can often translate into thinner margins if sellers try to beat each other on price. Higher ranked items may have less competition, but fewer sales. The question is, if you sell 10 widgets a day and profit $2 a piece on them or if you sell 1 premium gadget per day and profit $20, does it make a difference? At the end of the day it is net profit that pays the rent, not number of units sold.

Sometimes slower moving inventory can be just as profitable as the quick turn. A good example is books. Some people make a very nice living selling highly specialized books that are hard to find. They pick them up at a thrift shop or garage sale for a dollar or so and sell them for $20-200 or more. These books don't sell that often, but when they do, the profit margin is huge. You need to remember that your time to source, pack and ship inventory is valuable and sometimes it may be better to work smarter, not harder. Each individual seller needs to balance out the risk of having money tied up in slower moving inventory versus how much work they want to put into constantly replenishing fast moving inventory.

My strategy is to create a portfolio of a few fast, several medium, and a few slow moving products in my catalog. The rationale behind a mixed portfolio is to have a range of products so if more competitors move into your space for the top sellers in your catalog, you have time to source a new product while still continuing to make some sales. When you focus on hot sellers you will have to put more effort into staying competitive or continually sourcing products. If you want this to be any sort of lifestyle business, where you have some freedom to not always be working IN your business, you may want to consider the same. This also goes for mixing less expensive and more expensive items to balance out your inventory spending. It's almost like building an investment portfolio where you mix high risk high return stocks with low risk low return bonds.

So, after that lengthy explanation, determine whether each product is ranking well enough to make it a consideration. If your product is not listed, find some similar products and see how they are doing.

Tools to evaluate rank

As mentioned previously, sales rank is a reflection of when the item last sold. Every time an item sells it boosts the rank. When it doesn't sell for a while, the rank falls. So, if a bestselling item is out of stock for a while, rank can quickly dip. This is why we need to be able to track rank over time.

Keepa is a Chrome extension that tracks sales rank and price history. Once you install this extension, it inserts a graph right onto the product detail page on Amazon. If you click on it, you can find more information at their website. If you look at a product on Keepa you will see a spike in the sales rank graph whenever a product sells. What we don't know is whether those spikes were one sale or multiple sales. Checking how far apart these spikes occur over time however can give you insight into how often a product sells.

Check reviews

Check the reviews of the product or similar products. You absolutely want quality products that customers will love. Don't risk a high return rate or poor reviews by sourcing cheap (as in quality) products. If you want to sell cheap products, Amazon is not the platform for you. Make sure most people LOVE the products. You don't want to sell a wholesale product with an average of 3 stars or less.

If you are looking to private label however, products with 3 or less stars are an opportunity to bring to market a better product. You will want to do some additional research to make sure there are not a lot of other similar products that *are* getting 5 star reviews. If there isn't, this could be your golden opportunity to bring to market the product people are looking for that no one is giving them.

Check the competition

How many FBA sellers are on the same or similar listings? Everyone has different ideas about how many competitors they are willing to tolerate on the listing. From the product pages, click the Other Sellers On Amazon link to see all the offers for that product. Ask yourself:

- If there are FBA sellers (as indicated by the Prime symbol next to the price) on the first page, can I price competitively so that I show up on the first page of offers and still make the profit I want?

- If there are no FBA sellers on the first page, can I price so that I am competitive with the first 4-5 FBA sellers? You don't have to be the lowest price, but you should be somewhere in the first page with FBA sellers on it.

Ideally you don't want a lot of competition. It can be hard to find a good selling product without competition but if you are selling FBA, make sure you look at how many other FBA sellers there are. Merchant fulfilled sellers are not your competition. There are over a million PRIME members who will pick the seller that they can get PRIME shipping with. If you can get on the first page of FBA sellers, then it might be worth a trial order of that product to see how well it turns over. Also, if you are able to price within 2% of the Buy Box price you may get a turn in the Buy Box which helps sales dramatically.

If you are looking to private label the product, you want to make sure that there aren't tons of similar products already on the market. Some competition is good—it means someone has already done the market testing for you. A lot of competition means it may be hard to make it to the first page of search results on Amazon

When private labelling, you also want to ensure that there are no big name competitors. You don't want to go up against the big brand names in your niche.

If there are competing private label products, make sure they don't have tons of reviews. You can catch up to someone with 100 reviews or so, but 1000 reviews on an existing product will be harder to compete against.

Check the price history

Use CamelCamelCamel or Keepa to check price history. Both are available as Chrome extensions. CamelCamelCamel installs a button in your browser bar that you can click while on any Amazon product page and it will bring up a pop-up with the price history. Keepa's extension will place a price graph right in the product detail page on Amazon.

You are checking price history to ensure that the price you are seeing now is not an aberration—abnormally high or low. Check out the average price for the year. You want to be able to price your product competitively and still make a profit.

Check the market search volume

Use Merchant Words to determine the number of searches per month on Amazon. When you do a free search on Merchant Words, be sure to sort the results by Highest Search Volume so you see the top 3 keywords and their search volume.

Do a general keyword search on Google keyword planner to estimate web volume. On Google's tool, if you search with keywords that buyers use like buy, shopping, best, for sale, reviews, etc. you can gauge the number of searches with buying intent as opposed to those just looking for information.

You can run your product keywords on Google Trends and see how traffic is trending for this category. Is it growing or declining in popularity? Are there any seasonal spikes in interest? Can you capitalize on those spikes by having plenty of product in stock during those seasons?

Finally, you can also use Watchcount to check sales and the number of people watching the product on eBay. eBay serves a different clientele so take this information with a grain of salt. You are not comparing apples to apples. If nothing else, some people like to know that if their product tanked on Amazon that they could unload it on eBay.

Does the product have an expiry date/shelf life?

You want to be sure you can order in small enough quantities that you always have fresh product. Amazon has policies regarding shelf life and will either destroy expired inventory or you will have to pay to have them return it. I don't recommend perishable products for beginners.

Check the selling fees

Of the remaining products on your list that passed all of the above criteria, use Amazon's FBA calculator to determine a good estimate of the fees involved in selling that product. Write down the estimated fees and the current sell price (from the buy box as well as your lowest FBA competitor). Later, when you are sourcing you can add in your cost to buy the product and determine your estimated net profit. This step of calculating fees could be done after you determine cost of goods as well. You decide what works best for you but do not skip this step. Amazon fees can eat away a profit in a hurry so you need a good estimate of them.

The Next Steps

By this point you should have a pretty nice looking spreadsheet with lots of good data on it. Now we need to analyze it. The nice thing about using Excel for this is you can select any column you want and sort it by ascending and descending values. Select a column to analyze and from the Home tab click "Sort and Filter." You will be given the option to sort from smallest to largest or from largest to smallest value.

If you have not put your information in a spreadsheet, that is okay, you can just analyze your data manually.

I am assuming you are a beginner so let's start by looking for products with the lowest sales rank. Sort your sales rank column from lowest to highest. Now that your data is organized from best ranking to worst ranking, start at the top and look for any that meet most of these criteria too:

- Low sales rank (within the top 1% will sell the fastest)

- Not too many FBA competitors and ideally not Amazon itself

- A good amount of search traffic per month. How much will depend on how niche the item is but at least 1000 searches per month on Merchant Words would be my preference

- Well reviewed

- Can be sold for more than $10

Pick a few products that look the most promising and start sourcing them. If you come up empty handed, go back to your list and pick a few more products.

Chapter 4: Sourcing

Goal: Identify sources for your products and determine the cost to acquire them

The final step in product validation is determining the cost that you can acquire the goods for. Million dollar seller Jose Calero once said the profit is in the buying price, not the selling price. This can be tricky as a small business because when you are purchasing in smaller quantities you will get the least favorable wholesale price. You will also get discouraged when you discover that your wholesale cost is pretty close to what large sellers are retailing it for.

One strategy can be to order a small quantity first to test the market knowing that you may only break even. You can place a larger order to get a price break once you know the product can sell as well as how quickly it sells.

You can also try to order in quantities large enough to get free freight. Some suppliers will have a dollar threshold for free shipping, while others may have special offers from time to time. Make sure you are on your supplier's email list to get notifications of special offers. Remember, the profit is in reducing your cost of your goods.

What is a reasonable profit margin? Sellers vary as to what level of return they expect but averages are:

For wholesale: 15-35% with 20% typical

For private label: 30-50% with 40% typical

How to calculate profit margin
Step 1: Selling price-Amazon fees (including shipping to the warehouse)-Product cost (including shipping to you) = net profit.

Step 2: Net profit/selling price=percent margin

Example: Selling price is $20. Your cost to ship to Amazon's warehouse, seller's fees and FBA fees are roughly $6.50. Your net from Amazon is 13.50. The product cost you $9. $13.50 - $9= $4.50. This is your net profit. Your profit margin is net profit divided by selling price: 4.50/20=.225 or 22.5%

As a general rule of thumb look for a product that you can purchase for roughly 1/3 the retail price. That is, you want to be able to list it for three times (3X) your purchase price. Fees and shipping will eat up roughly 1/3 and the other 1/3 is your profit. The higher the selling price of the item, the more you can afford 2X markup (i.e. where the wholesale cost is half of the retail price) instead of 3X as certain fulfillment fees are fixed. On a lower priced item, for example $10, at least $3-4 will be fees so on a product that costs you $3 you may only make $3. On a $50 item your fees may be $11 so if your product cost is $25 you can still profit $14.

Heavy or oversized items may incur more fees so leave yourself room and always start with a small test order to see what your net profit actually is before investing in more inventory. Until you actually sell one, you won't know the actual cost to sell, just an estimate.

Tip: When estimating Amazon fees use the FBA revenue calculator. If your exact item is in the Amazon catalog, use that to get a good estimate of fees. If you item is not in the Amazon catalog, use a similar product to estimate fees.

Caution: There are some unscrupulous sellers who may inflate the weight of an item in the product listing page. These sellers are merchant fulfilling and trying to get a larger shipping allowance to squeeze a few more cents of profit from the sale. This hurts FBA sellers because some of the FBA fee is based on the weight of the item. It is a good idea to check the product weights in the listing from time to time and make sure they are accurate or you may pay too much in fees.

Tip: If you use some sort of spreadsheet or software to keep track of your inventory, you may want to add a column for weight. Once the item ships to Amazon's warehouse you won't be able to check the weight.

Types of suppliers
Depending on the product, you can look for wholesalers, suppliers, and sales reps or you can try to go straight to the manufacturer.

Manufacturers are the companies that actually make the product. They may sell directly to businesses or they may use distributors or sales reps. Generally, if you buy goods from the source you will get the best price because you eliminate any middle men. The downside is you may be expected to make large minimum purchases. If you are doing private label, you will want to work with a manufacturer who can make customizations to your product.

Wholesalers and Distributors carry products that they purchase from the manufacturer. They then sell these products to businesses. They may carry products from multiple manufacturers. This means you could buy multiple products from one supplier. This can save you money on shipping as well as make it easier to meet minimum order requirements. Sometimes these companies are buying in large enough volume that their wholesale prices are similar to what you can do direct from the manufacturer as a small business. For beginners, you will probably only have enough startup capital to work with wholesalers and distributors. Some companies have minimum orders as low as $100.

Sales reps usually represent one or more product lines. They are a middle man between manufacturers and retailers. If you are sourcing from abroad a similar role is played by the sourcing agent. A sourcing agent will take your request for a product and find factories that can produce it. These agents usually work on a commission.

Pick a product from your list and start looking for sources.

Google the name of your product along with words like bulk, wholesale, supplier, or distributor. Spend a little time going through several pages of results until the results start to become irrelevant. Many of the best sources have very basic websites that do not bother with trying to rank in Google so they won't be on the first page of search results. In fact, there is a good chance that the top results aren't true wholesalers but rather retailers who do bulk discounts.

Other keywords to try in combination with your product keywords include minimum order, login to see prices, resale certificate, tax exempt certificate, and sales rep. These are common words you will find on a true wholesaler's site. If your results seem irrelevant, trying putting the phrases in quotation marks. For example, "plush rabbit" and "log in to see prices" would be a search to find wholesalers of plush rabbits. Be sure to include the word *and* in between your two search terms so that Google knows you want results with exact matches for both of these phrases.

Tip: Use those same keywords in a Google Image search to make quick work of visually finding your product. Just hover over any image in the results and you will see what site it is from so you can easily assess whether it is a potential wholesale source. Click on the image and you will be offered a link that takes you to the page the image is from. This is my favorite way to quickly find the products I want because I can just look at the pictures.

You can also search wholesale or manufacturers directories such as Thomasnet in the US, Indiamart for India, and Alibaba, Global Sources, or Made-in-China (with hyphens) for Asia and beyond. Domestic wholesale directories include WholesaleCentral and Toptenwholesale.com. Be sure to research any company you find through these sites as they are just a platform to help you find companies but don't vet them for you. Other paid services such as Worldwide Brands and Salehoo do vet the suppliers in their directory.

Other ways to find suppliers

- As I mentioned earlier, if you can find a local company you will save a bunch on shipping if they allow will call. You can use your local yellow pages or an online search. Use your product keyword plus the name of your city and/or state.

- Look up the product online on retail e-commerce sites or find it in a store and look on the packaging for the company name and location. Do an online search for that company.

- Twitter: Search for keywords in the category you want such as "kitchen supplier." Don't use hashtags, just search the words. Anything with those words in the description or in a tweet will display in the results. Scroll through and you are likely to find some smaller companies you haven't heard of—even if you already know your niche! These smaller companies may have some interesting products that could be the next PooPourri.

- You can also start a Twitter account for your niche of choice. This is a long term approach, but start following people in your niche and over time companies will start approaching you. I have found companies both through them following me and by them direct messaging me. Again, this takes some time but cultivating a list in your niche is not just about finding the occasional source, but has the fringe benefit of building an interested audience you can market to when your product comes out.

Ideal qualities in a wholesale source

Your ideal source does not sell retail themselves. You will never be able to compete with your source if it comes down to price. You will occasionally find some exceptions. I have one wholesale source that sells retail but their retail prices are at least 3X markup.

Make sure the company is offering legitimate wholesale prices and not just offering a bulk discount. I have seen some companies that offer a "wholesale discount" of 2.5% if you buy $250 or more all the way up to a whopping 7% discount if you by $3000 or more. You don't want this!!

The word "wholesale" has become somewhat of a marketing term in recent years. Many retailers advertise prices that are "wholesale to the public" but their prices aren't really wholesale. As a general guideline, wholesale price should be no more than 2/3 of the retail price.

A website that requires you to login to see wholesale prices is one sign that this is a legitimate wholesale business. Another good sign is if the business requires you to register with your state resale certificate. This means the general public won't have access to wholesale prices. A state re-sale certificate is sometimes also referred to as a tax exempt certificate.

Check your wholesale prices against the market—look at what other online retailers are selling the product for. I once signed up for a wholesale account because I wanted to carry a certain small appliance this company carried. They were the name given to me by the manufacturer as their authorized distributor for the western U.S. I could get the product for $38.99 from them and the retail was around $60. I did a little searching and found some online companies selling this same product for $43! After fees, I would have lost money!

Other types of sources:

Some people do very well sourcing from liquidators. There are online liquidators, as well as brick and mortar liquidators in most mid to large size cities. Some search terms include liquidator, closeout, and salvage. These products can be shelf pulls, customer returns, and closeouts.

You must be cautious with this strategy. It can be very enticing for the beginner because of the low cost per unit. You must ask yourself a few questions though:

- Why are these items being liquidated? Were they not successfully selling in the store? Did the manufacturer make too many (which may mean there is a surplus of these in the marketplace)?

- If the items are shelf pulls or returns are they in good sellable condition? Do not sell something as "new" on Amazon unless it is *and* looks perfectly new. That includes the packaging. Anything less than perfect should be sold on eBay instead.

Buying from overseas:

We will discuss sourcing from overseas a little more in the private label section but if you just want to purchase generic products from overseas, bear in mind the following:

- Always order a sample (or a few) to check the quality of the item

- Do not buy anything associating itself with a name brand or resembling a name brand product. Cheap knockoffs (i.e.

fake products) abound and selling them is one great way to get your Amazon seller account suspended.

- Do not assume that the products meet codes for your country. You are responsible for making sure that any applicable standards for your country are met (e.g. FDA regulations, FCC or ISO Standards).

- Are these same products being offered direct to the consumer from overseas? There are more and more international sellers on eBay and Amazon and if they are able to sell directly to customers at a similar price as your wholesale price you may have trouble competing.

Sourcing Private Label

This could be a book in itself, and if you plan to source from China, there are books specifically dealing with that. I highly recommend that if you want to source from China that you check out www.chineseimporting.com and their associated eBook.

Caution: Be careful when sourcing private label products that you are not copying someone else's products. Especially check for patents or patent pending. Remember, inspiration not imitation.

Sourcing from China can especially come with risks and I have seen a few products on Alibaba that I absolutely recognize the US company that sells it under their name. Avoid anything that you recognize and do an extra careful search of any product you are sourcing to ensure that it is not patented by anyone else. Some suppliers are so eager for your business that they may not honor any agreements they have made with another company and tell you they have the right to sell you a certain product. Beware that this works both ways—if you have a supplier from overseas custom manufacture a product for you they may turn around and sell it to someone else or even list it themselves.

Google Image search can be one way to find other instances of the manufacturer's images (using good keywords). You can look for matching images to see who else is selling that product. Look at any companies carrying that same product and evaluate whether they may have protected that product. The last thing you want is to be sitting on hundreds of units that you can't sell because of patent infringement Hire a pro to do your patent research if need be, especially before sinking a lot of funds into a large order. If you must do it yourself, you can search USPTO.

With those warnings out of the way...

Finding private label manufacturers:

For starters, do an internet search for the type of product you are looking for + private label or white label as your keywords. For example, lip balm private label or energy bars private label.

You can also search manufacturer directories:

*Thomasnet in North America

*IndiaMart for India

*Alibaba, Aliexpress, DHGate, Made-In-China, HKTDC, and Global Sources for Asia and beyond

Reverse Lookup: Find a product that you like and check the packaging for where it was made. For example, I have a particular travel mug that I really like and noticed the name of the company on the bottom. I looked them up online, and sure enough they offer a range of products that can be customized.

An easy, but not always cheap way to private label:

Look for gift or promotional product businesses. These are the types of businesses that will put your company logo on just about anything. You know, like the polo shirt that you got from your company golf tournament, the comb you got from the hairdresser with their name on it, the travel mug that your university sells in the bookstore.

Many of these products can be found on Alibaba as well, but you can pay a little extra for the convenience and security of working with a domestic source. Using these companies can be one way to market test your product with a low minimum order. You can always look for someone manufacturing the same product on Alibaba later when you know you want to keep producing the product.

If you have a particular product in mind, search the product name with the words "promotional product" or "custom imprint." Or you can do a more general search for "promotional products."

If you decide to go this route, please bear in mind a few pointers:

- Order a sample first. Some products are great quality, but others are not. Remember that the intent of these products is as giveaways or gifts to clients or prospective clients so they are not always retail worthy.

- Have a professional logo or artwork made for your project and upload it. Some companies have their own designers but if you ever want to take your project to another manufacturer you will want the full rights to use your existing artwork.

Consider private labelling domestically:

You may be able to do this especially in Health, Personal Care, Beauty, and Grocery categories.

Pros:

- You may be able to fall back on the manufacturer's product liability (but still check with your lawyer if you need your own)

- Reduced chance of scams or knock offs by sourcing domestically—companies are more likely to respect non-disclosure agreements and contracts. That said, never assume that just because a company is domestic that it is legitimate.

- May be less expensive to ship

- Communication in English

- No customs, duty, or freight forwarding to worry about or pay for

- Can market "Made in USA" or whatever country you are living in

Cons:

- May be harder to source some items

- More expensive product cost but may be offset by fewer costs like shipping and customs clearance

- May need to order in larger quantities

Once you find a supplier, domestic or overseas, you will want to find out some basic information such as:

- What is their minimum order quantity?

- What is the per unit cost and at what quantities can you get price breaks?

- What is their lead time (how long do they need to make the product)?

How many can they produce per month (if your product becomes a smash hit you want your supplier to have the capacity to keep up with demand)?

What are the shipping options? If you are shipping from overseas, your choices are by air (e.g. DHL), by air freight (airport to airport), or by sea (port to port). Don't be alarmed by high shipping fees. Think of shipping costs in relation to your product cost. If you order 500 units and pay $250 in shipping that only adds .50 to the cost of each unit.

If your product is unique, will they sign a non-disclosure agreement? Will they agree not to sell your product to other companies (applies to products that you have modified or designed yourself, not to generic products the company already has in their catalog)?

You do not need to ask all of these questions in your initial contact, but they should be addressed at some point in your communications with any supplier you are seriously considering.

Additional questions to ask yourself are:

Do you need a customs broker? A freight forwarder? Investigate the costs of duty and customs if you are importing products from another country. If you work with a customs broker, they can assist you with estimates. You can also attempt to look up the information yourself on the government website http://hts.usitc.gov/. Factor these costs into your total product cost.

Putting it all together, the final analysis

Once you have found some suppliers and have received some quotes, add your estimated cost of goods to your spreadsheet and do one last analysis. You may choose to sort your columns by net profit (highest to lowest), rank (lowest to highest), and number of competitors (lowest to highest). An ideal product will be:

- Low in rank

- High in net profit

- Have few competitors

Finding the ideal product is like winning the lottery so don't panic if none of the products fit the bill exactly. Use your noodle and pick the product(s) that come closest. Make this a cold, business decision and not a personal one. Which products numbers look the best?

Okay, now for the scariest and most exciting part:

Pick a product!! Remember you are not married to the product you pick so just start. Too many people get stuck on finding that perfect product and they end up doing nothing at all. Don't be that person. Pick something and make a small investment. Your inventory is an asset and you are unlikely to lose your entire investment even if it wasn't the right product. Remember, you can always drop your price or sell it on eBay. The important thing to remember is you will have zero success until you take action.

Chapter 5: Samples and test marketing

Goal: Order trial quantities of your chosen product(s) and determine if they sell, how quickly, and at what actual profit.

Now that you have made a decision on a product, start with the smallest order you can. Order 2-3 samples and check for quality and consistency. Adopt the restaurant maxim "If you aren't proud of it, don't serve it." Make sure the products you choose are ones that you are proud to sell.

You absolutely want quality. Amazon's customers are not just looking for cheap prices—you will get bad reviews so don't risk it by going for cheap quality. If you ordered a few samples, try listing a couple and see how quickly they sell. If they sell, try ordering a little more. Your profit here may be slim, but that is okay for now. Set the price you will sell at and see if the price works. As you make larger bulk orders, your cost of goods will go down and your profit margin increases. The point here is to test if it will sell and how quickly before investing too much capital. You will save money in the long run. The best and most accurate product research comes from the data you get from actually selling the product.

If you are sourcing from China, an easy way to get samples is to order from Aliexpress, DHgate, or even eBay. If you search eBay for 'gold watch China' you can often find the same products as are found on Alibaba and Aliexpress but at better prices. You also have eBay buyer protection. If you are going to try this method, ask the seller if they are a trade company (basically a wholesaler) or the manufacturer. If you find a product you like you will want to be able to order in larger quantities and request customizations.

If your small run of trial products sell, keep track of your sales per week or sales per day and use this data use to determine how big your next order should be. If you are buying domestically from a wholesaler you may want to stock 4-6 weeks' worth of inventory. If you are ordering from overseas it may take 4-8 weeks to restock so order enough to cover at least 2 months. Perishable items should have a quick turnaround.

Ultimately, you want to find a balance where you are ordering in large enough quantities to get the best prices but not so much that your cash is tied up for 6 months while they sell. You will usually save on shipping costs if you order less frequently and some wholesalers offer free shipping on larger orders. With some companies free shipping can be on orders as low as $250+, while some are $500 and beyond. If you have the storage space available, you may not want to send all of your inventory to Amazon at once (of the same item). If the items sell slowly, you may be faced with long term storage fees if it sits in the warehouse for too long. Watch your reports in Seller Central and aim to send in no more than 6 months' worth of inventory. Note that long term storage fees only apply to items for which you have 2 or more in the warehouse.

If you are ordering from a manufacturer, most should let you order samples followed by a test order but after that you may be asked to order minimum order quantity (MOQ). You can try to negotiate and if they are hungry for your business they may work with you. Be aware that manufacturers that are used to working with larger companies may not be as willing to be flexible.

Whatever the case, my philosophy is to start small and build from there. Test the market and let your profits increase as your cost of goods goes down with bulk discounts.

So, that officially ends this book—there are more ideas for finding products and sources after this conclusion but I want to wrap up what we have learned so far before filling your brain with other ideas for finding products.

Summary

Choose some categories you may want to sell in

Use the suggestions in Chapter 1 to look for product ideas—don't censor your list at this point, just get ideas.

Validate your ideas—check each potential product against the criteria we discussed and cross off any that don't fit the criteria.

Find sources for your products and estimate potential profits. If you are private labelling from overseas, make sure you double check patents as well as the need for product liability insurance and compliance with quality standards.

Buy a few samples to check for quality. Try listing them to see how quickly they sell. One strategy might be to pick 2-3 products from your list and buy samples for all of them. Test selling them all at once. Reorder the most promising one(s) in a larger quantity.

If you are doing private label, promote your product (outside the scope of this book)

Once your first product is selling with minimal promotion and intervention on your part, repeat and build yourself a catalog of diverse products. Aim for a mix of fast and not so fast movers as well as a range of price points. Diversification is the best protection for your business.

Some parting advice:

Start as small as you need to and reinvest your profits until you get to the level you want to be at. Find the balance of work vs. profit. Remember that if you want to net $5,000 a month you will have to sell roughly $15-20,000 in product every month. This means you will be spending about $5-7,000 a month in inventory. You also need to process this inventory (label and ship) or hire someone to do it for you. At some point, you cross a line between an easy little source of extra income to it becoming a job. Most people are not looking to replace their day job with another job that is just as time consuming or tedious. They are looking for some freedom. Find the level that works for your lifestyle and your income needs. Good luck!

Still stuck? More ways to find product ideas and sources

Subscribe to magazines from B2B sites: HKTDC is a Hong Kong Based B2B platform with several niche magazines http://www.hktdc.com/mis/pm/en/HKTDC-Product-Magazines.html

Promotional products: bags, cups, blankets, corkscrews, t-shirts—all can have a logo or design printed on it. We already talked about this as a simple way to private label products domestically. But instead of imprinting it with your brand you can create merchandise that appeals to a niche-for example nurses, gardeners or bikers. People that are passionate about their hobbies or professions tend to buy all sorts of silly things because they relate to their niche. Remember that whole series of license plate holders "Nurses do it with Care" or "Aerospace Engineers do it with lift and thrust"? Pick a niche you are familiar with and create some humorous products or slogans around that.

Houzz.com: Look through the idea books and marketplace for product ideas and what people are saving. Each product also has a section in the sidebar for "People who liked this product also liked."

Look at Consumers Reports, Cooks Illustrated and other magazines that test and review new products: Be sure to pick the top rated items!! Also check websites like Product Wiki or Bootic where users add rating information. Pick a category, sort by bestselling or popularity, and filter price range if you want.

Open your eyes and ears: This may seem obvious to some of you but pay attention to what others are buying, wearing, etc. For example, rosaries as necklaces on teenagers was popular last year while a few years ago it was stretchy saint bracelets. Listen for the magic words "I wish they made…" from both yourself and others. Look around your house for ideas. What about staples like toilet paper, garbage bags, tape…things people need to replenish but don't expire or go bad. Think boring—some of the products that are highly ranked are mundane things like rings for your shower curtain.

Join Facebook groups related to your niche and lurk: Do NOT use these as a way to conduct market research or you will get the boot pretty quickly. Rather, listen to what problems people have, what products they like, and what they are looking for.

Make a bundle: Bundling can be as good or better than private label. You create the listing and usually are the only seller but you don't have to hassle with all of the details of private label because you are using other people's products. Don't just pair random things, make it useful. Maybe a set of supplies for a dorm room. Perhaps a set of supplies for keeping your pool clean. Be unique and be hard to copy. People that are low enough to hijack your listings are too lazy and likely too cheap to go through the trouble of copying all of the details. If they don't copy it exactly, you can have them removed from the listing. Try sourcing your bundled items from different manufacturers or include one item that is your branded product. You can also bundle your product with a local product—for example locally produced honey with a honey dripper. Be sure to read Amazon's bundling policies at Seller Central.

Go shopping: I know that sounds simplistic but really, browse the aisles looking for interesting products. Pick them up and read the label—who makes them? Make a note of it and go home and validate for Amazon.

Go to Trend hunter.com and browse through articles: Look for articles such as top 100 gadget trends for August. Also be sure to search by category.

After a trade show, search for reports and roundups on blogs: Potential keywords for this type of search would be the name of the trade show + the year + product category or keyword. For example, try searching Toy Fair New York 2015 Games and look at some of the posts that come up.

Think seasonally: Not just holidays, but what do you need when the weather gets cold, gets hot, what do you need in the summer (camping, gardening), what do you need in the winter (gifts and toys, ice scrapers, scarves, mittens, bikini wraps for that Caribbean cruise!). For holidays, think beyond the obvious. What about a set of pumpkin carving tools, or hooks to hang Christmas lights with? Turkey basters, butchers twine, and meat thermometers might work well at Thanksgiving.

Think about what you can get in your locality that is not available nationally: There is lots of opportunity here. For example, Trader Joes is not in every locality nor is Sephora (watch out for restricted brands). It doesn't need to be store brands. What if you are a scrapbooker that lives 50 miles from the nearest Michaels? What if you are a cooking aficionado and can't find French green lentils in your local grocery store? If you live in an urban or suburban area you are at an advantage. What might someone in a smaller town not be able to get in their town and need to order online? If you are travelling, pay attention when you are in a smaller town to what kind of stores they have and what items they cannot easily come by. This is really a gold mine because there are so many small towns in North America that are miles and miles from an urban center. If you live in a small town, you already know what you can't find locally!

Think about perpetual problems: Health and fitness, diet and weight loss, antiaging, and making money/reducing debt are all perpetual problems that people will spend money on over and over because they are looking for an EASIER or MORE EFFECTIVE solution than the last one they tried.

Look for ideas on Etsy: You may also find products to source directly on Etsy. I have heard stories of people approaching Etsy sellers to either carry their products or even do private label for them! You just need to politely ask (and don't be offended if they politely refuse, not every artist on Etsy wants to mass produce their products). If you can make a handmade version of your product own idea you might be able to market test it on Etsy before investing in custom manufacturing. Sign up for the Etsy newsletters to get curated finds delivered to your inbox that will give your inspiration.

Consider bilingual products: Recently I was at Walgreens and noticed a small shelf area with a random assortment of products on it. At first I thought they might be clearance, but upon closer inspection I realized they were products aimed at Spanish speakers. Some were imported, but others were ordinary personal care products that had packaging with both English and Spanish on it. If you are doing private label, think of the marketing advantage if your private label product had bilingual packaging and instructions.

And speaking of ethnicity: Think about tools, foods, candies, or beauty products that could be imported that certain ethnic groups might want. My background is Dutch and I go to stores that carry Dutch licorice, toasts, chocolate sprinkles, mints, etc. all of which are not available at regular grocery stores in my area. I have also bought a special waffle iron to make stroep wafels. My husband is of Norwegian descent and he bought a pastry cloth for rolling out lefse. What is your ethnic background and what sorts of products could you source that would appeal to your ethnicity? Remember that these specialty items may not be available in many areas of the country and so for many shoppers can only be found online.

Well, there you have it. Hopefully I have given you plenty of ideas for finding winning products. Once again, I wish you all the best in your e-commerce journey.

Before you go, I would like to ask a quick favor from you. Can I ask you to say a few words about this book in a review? Like Amazon sellers, Kindle authors rely on genuine reviews from readers to help others find this book (reviews are one factor that help your product appear higher in search results—remember that when you have your product live on Amazon!!). I would truly appreciate it.

Appendix A:

Should you sell products in the top 100? A rant

The quick answer is…possibly. But before you leap, consider the following:

How many courses, books, videos, websites, etc. have taught you to troll the top 100? How many thousands of students or viewers have been taught this? Granted, many people who learn about this business won't actually follow through, but still, how many hundreds or thousands will follow through, even if just to try it? What does this mean for the number of competitors you will have—not just at this moment, but in the coming weeks and months? Everybody wants that one, single product that will sell 10 a day, but the reality is we won't all achieve it.

How many people are using the top 100 to find products to private label? As multiple similar products emerge it will dilute the number of sales any particular product will have. Many people playing the private label game come from an internet marketing background. They know marketing on the web and they know how to sell, don't set yourself up for discouragement by trying to go up against the big boys on highly competitive products. You can tackle that later when you have more experience yourself.

For every potential private label product in the top 100 that looks like it has great rank and low competition, how many people are actively sourcing that product right now that you don't know about? If you are ordering from overseas by the time you get your first order in 30-60 days, there may be 10 more people with listings up.

The Best Sellers list is fluid so it can be influenced by seasonality, a product being featured in a magazine or blog, a fad with unknown life span (e.g. alkaline water)—you don't always know how long an item has been in the bestsellers list.

I don't want to discourage you by pointing all of this out, but I want you to be aware of these considerations so you don't have unreasonable expectations. While it may be easier and certainly enticing to sell 100+ per month of a single product and only have to source that one product, the competition will see your success and try to pick off some of your action. All the gurus are teaching *you* to pick off part of someone else's action, what is stopping the next wave of people from taking some of *yours*?? Let's quickly do the math:

Seller A sells 500 units per month; seller B and C come along and steal some of their customers. Now seller A may have 300 sales, and B and C have grabbed 100 each. Next, seller D through K see seller A's success and they join in with their product. Now seller A has 150 sales, B and C have 50 each and D through K have 30 each.

The short term success may be there, but as soon as someone sees you are successful, they will become your competitor.

Also, when it comes to private label, let's learn a lesson from another big player, Google. How many successful websites have lost their income overnight due to Google updates? Google does their best to reward legitimate, useful websites and weed out the spammy stuff. How long before Amazon sees that 20 people are selling the exact same silicone baking mat under their own name and puts the kibosh on that? People think that slapping your name on a product protects them somehow but there are already stories circulating of private label sellers who have had other sellers jump on their listing with the exact same unbranded product. Amazon's perspective has been that if it is an identical product, the listing can and should be shared. Amazon is different from eBay in that they only want one listing per item. Private label as some are teaching it is gaming the system—put your name on it so you can create your own listing that no one else can use. In the history of the internet, people that game the system may win temporarily, but they usually lose in the long run. The behemoth, in this case Amazon, will always win. They have the money and it is their sandbox we are playing in. I can assure you Amazon does not want people messing up their catalog with 20 listings for identical products, even if they each have their name stamped on the packaging. Play by the rules, do what seems right and you will win in the long term.

I wish you all the best in your business!

Made in the USA
San Bernardino, CA
12 February 2019